W9-BPL-173

NAVY SEALS

SPECIAL FORCES: PROTECTING, BUILDING, TEACHING, AND FIGHTING

NAVY SEALS

by Jack Montana

Mason Crest Publishers

MASON CREST PUBLISHERS INC.
370 Reed Road
Broomall, Pennsylvania 19008
(866)MCP-BOOK (toll free)
www.masoncrest.com

First Printing
9 8 7 6 5 4 3 2 1

Library of Congress Cataloging-in-Publication Data

Montana, Jack.
 Navy SEALs / by Jack Montana.
    p. cm.
 Includes bibliographical references and index.
 ISBN 978-1-4222-1843-3
 ISBN (series) 978-1-4222-1836-5
 1. United States. Navy. SEALs—Juvenile literature. I. Title.
 VG87.M66 2011
 359.9'84—dc22
                            2010021842

Produced by Harding House Publishing Service, Inc.
www.hardinghousepages.com
Interior design by MK Bassett-Harvey.
Cover design by Torque Advertising + Design.
Printed in USA by Bang Printing.

With thanks and appreciation to the U.S. Military for the use of information, text, and images.

Contents

Introduction

lite forces are the tip of Freedom's spear. These small, special units are universally the first to engage, whether on reconnaissance missions into denied territory for larger conventional forces or in direct action, surgical operations, preemptive strikes, retaliatory action, and hostage rescues. They lead the way in today's war on terrorism, the war on drugs, the war on transnational unrest, and in humanitarian operations as well as nation building. When large-scale warfare erupts, they offer theater commanders a wide variety of unique, unconventional options.

Most such units are regionally oriented, acclimated to the culture and conversant in the languages of the areas where they operate. Since they deploy to those areas regularly, often for combined training exercises with indigenous forces, these elite units also serve as peacetime "global scouts," and "diplomacy multipliers," beacons of hope for the democratic aspirations of oppressed peoples all over the globe.

Elite forces are truly "quiet professionals": their actions speak louder than words. They are self-motivated, self-confidant, versatile, seasoned, mature individuals who rely on teamwork more than daring-do. Unfortunately, theirs is dangerous work. Since the 1980 attempt to rescue hostages from the U.S. embassy in Tehran, American special operations forces have suffered casualties in real-world operations at close to fifteen times the rate of U.S. conventional forces. By the very nature of the challenges that face special operations forces, training for these elite units has proven even more hazardous.

Thus it's with special pride that I join you in saluting the brave men who volunteer to serve in and support these magnificent units and who face such difficult challenges ahead.

—*Colonel John T. Carney, Jr., USAF–Ret.*
President, Special Operations Warrior Foundation

CHAPTER 1

The History of the Navy

The U.S. Navy performs many different tasks, but every mission has to do with one of the following: winning wars, deterring aggression, or maintaining freedom of the seas. The U.S. Navy is currently the world's strongest naval power.

When you consider that 70 percent of the world is covered in water, 80 percent of the planet's population lives close to a coastal area, and 90 percent of the exchange of goods takes place over the seas, you can understand why the United States needs a strong navy. What's more, the world has become more interconnected. Every day we use goods that were carried over sea to America. For the United States to stay powerful, it is easy to see that a strong navy must be maintained.

The Navy performs their missions to:

- Serve as guardians for America's freedom and defend the American way.
- Support the freedoms held dear in other countries, promoting peace and stability.
- Ensure goods travel safely on a global scale.

The Navy performs missions in the air and on land, as well as at sea. A sailor in the Navy might participate in a peacekeeping mission—or he might see gunfire in combat. She might end up in the cockpit of a F018—or in the control-room of a nuclear submarine. Where the military is needed, the Navy is present.

HISTORY

The Navy has defended America since the Revolutionary War. At America's beginning, the establishment of an official navy was debated, supporters thought a navy would protect trade and defend America's coast. At first, individual colonies owned their own ships; then, when the **federal** government took ownership of the ships and added two more, the U.S. Navy was officially created. October 13, 1775, is now known as the U.S. Navy's official birthday.

UNDERSTAND THE FULL MEANING

federal: Pertaining to the nation, as opposed to individual states.

U.S. Navy Admiral James Stavridis, Supreme Allied Commander Europe, visits sailors and Marines during the Navy birthday celebration at Camp Leatherneck, Afghanistan, October 13, 2009.

Signalmen of Union Navy Rear Admiral John A. Dahlgren's flagship receiving a message from the Georgia shore during the Civil War.

At first, however, the United States did not develop the Navy and did not have a strong, organized force of ships to defend it. A wake-up call came when American ships were unable to stop a blockade by the British in the War of 1812. In the Mexican-American War, the Navy tasted victory, however, and successfully completed a mission in which 12,000 army troops landed with equipment in one day at Veracruz, Mexico, leading to the city's surrender. This was the Navy's first mission of this sort, an operation incorporating both land and naval forces together.

While the Navy did not see much combat during World War I, it grew in strength under the Naval Act of 1916. Battleships and aircraft carriers were built. The United States became a rising power, and a modern Navy was necessary for this. Starting the Navy SEAL Special Forces team was an important part of updating the capabilities of the Navy for twentieth-century military conflicts.

CHAPTER 2
The History of the Navy SEALs

The U.S. Navy SEALs are the ultimate modern warriors. The name stands for Sea, Air, Land; in other words, the SEALs can fight in any environment. But they are best known for their ability to survive and fight in the water.

The story of the Navy SEALs during World War II and after shows the changing role Special Forces had in defeating **fascist** and **communist** uprisings. The SEALs' story is also the story of American involvement in the world since the mid-twentieth century.

UNDERSTAND THE FULL MEANING

fascist: Related to the government system in which a dictator has complete control, such as in World War II Germany and Italy.

communist: Related to an economic system that limits individual rights and freedoms.

WORLD WAR II

During World War II the Military needed troops to assist the Navy in deploying land troops on beaches. The Amy and Navy established the Amphibious Scout and Raider School in Fort Pierce, Florida. An early version of the SEAL team helped the invasion of North Africa in 1942.

President John F. Kennedy (a World War II Navy veteran) foresaw the need for a trained force to fight **unconventional warfare** in future overseas conflicts. He increased funding for Special Operations units and invested 100 million dollars in Special Forces units. Areligh Burke, Chief of Naval Operations, recommended **guerilla** and anti-guerilla units. He wanted those units to be able to operate on sea, air, or land.

The military began basic SEAL indoctrination-training classes. Soldiers learned to fight hand-to-hand combat, fly in high-altitude parachuting, and set up demolition devices, while they also studied foreign languages. The first SEAL

UNDERSTAND THE FULL MEANING

unconventional warfare: Warfare in which unusual means are used.

guerilla: Military tactics in which a small force of soldiers uses raids and ambushes against a larger force.

Cold War: A state of political hostility between countries in which there is no armed conflict.

arms race: Two or more countries engaged in a competition over the size and destructive power of their weapons' capabilities.

teams were commissioned in 1962. Since the beginning, the Navy SEALs achieved excellence in all they did.

Warfare would continue after the Second World War. The **Cold War** brought with it the threat of nuclear weapons. Special Forces teams like the Navy SEALs were there to meet the challenge.

The First SEAL

Roy H. Boehm enlisted in the Navy in April 1941 and fought the Japanese from February 1942 until 1945. He survived one of the largest sea battles of World War II. While he served the U.S. Navy, Boehm had attained the following skills: deep sea diving, emergence rescue chamber operator, and underwater demolition expertise. He also assisted the Navy in creating its first counterinsurgency course. In 1961, he was first Officer in Charge of the first SEAL team.

"The only easy day was yesterday."

—unofficial NAVY SEALs motto

HOT MISSIONS IN THE COLD WAR

The Marines' task in the Cold War was to combat communist revolutions from Southeast Asia to the Caribbean. The U.S. SEALs fought against the growing threat of communism wherever it sprung up. The strategy was this: if the United States could beat the larger powers in an **arms race** while

Navy SEALs painted their faces green during their missions in the Vietnam war, so their faces would blend in with the jungle around them.

crushing rebellions in colonial powers, then they could eventually win the Cold War.

MEN WITH GREEN FACES: SEALS IN VIETNAM

The history of Vietnam goes back to the mid-nineteenth century when the French conquered Indochina. The French established colonial rule in Vietnam for the next seven decades. Viet Cong forces, led by general Ho Chi Menh, began the "August Revolution," a collection of popular movements revolting against what was already eighty years of colonial rule. In September 1945, Ho Chi Menh proclaimed the Democratic Republic of Vietnam a "free and independent country," and quoted the American Declaration of Independence in his speech. After the battle of Dien Bien Phu in May of 1954, the Northern Vietnamese ended the French occupation. The American Army stepped into the power vacuum to defend the South Vietnamese from what they saw as Communist aggression.

In March 1962 the SEALs began operations to train the South Vietnamese army. The SEALs taught the South Vietnamese forces how to fight guerilla tactics. Meanwhile, the North Vietnamese relied on conflicts between the civilian population and the regular army, using ambush and sabotage to magnify the element of surprise. Guerilla warfare depends on striking a vulnerable target and then withdrawing almost immediately. Unlike conventional warfare, in

UNDERSTAND THE FULL MEANING

colonial: Referring to the system where a powerful, developed country controls an undeveloped one.

which two enemies fire from far away, the SEALs battled the Viet Cong in closer range, often inches away.

The CIA also used the SEALs in secret operations, which included targeting North Vietnamese Army leaders and Viet Cong sympathizers for capture and assassination. The SEALs developed highly effective strategies in combating guerillas. Over two hundred enemies died for every SEAL

SEALs faced dangerous guerilla warfare situations in Vietnam, and were often forced to find ways to survive in enemy territory.

Profile of Courage: Thomas Norris

Thomas Norris joined the Navy hoping to fly. Due to problems with his vision, he trained to become a Navy SEAL instead. He struggled during training, and instructors discussed taking him off of the course—but he graduated from training.

In April 1972, he rescued two pilots stuck in enemy territory after their aircraft went out of commission. He led five men 2,000 meters (1.24 miles). Finally, they found one of the pilots at dawn and returned to their base. The next day, after surviving a savage rocket attack on their base, Norris led three men on two more unsuccessful attempts for the other pilot.

Two days after they found the first soldier, an aircraft scout reported seeing the pilot. Wearing traditional Vietnamese clothing, Norris and his men drifted down river, using a wooden Vietnamese boat. They found the pilot in the early morning and returned, avoiding a Viet Cong patrol. Close to their base, they came under intense gunfire. Norris called an airstrike and was able to escape under smoke deployed by the aircraft.

Six months later Norris received a head wound that nearly killed him. Michael Thornton courageously saved Norris and received the Medal of Honor for his actions. He was the first person to receive the Medal of Honor for saving the life of another Medal of Honor recipient. Both were able to witness each other's Medal of Honor ceremonies.

Norris retired from the Navy and joined the FBI.

Members of a SEAL team move down the Bassac River in a SEAL team assault boat during operations along the river south of Saigon in Vietnam in 1967.

lost. The Viet Cong called the SEALs "men with green faces" due to their camouflage.

In 1968, the Viet Cong began a major operation against the South Vietnamese called the "Tet Offensive." The North Vietnamese hoped it would drive a stake into the heart of the American army, comparable to the battle of Dien Bien Phu. While the Tet Offensive damaged American morale, the Viet Cong suffered many casualties.

In 1970, Richard Nixon began his plan of "Vietnamization," which would give responsibility for defense to the South Vietnamese and remove U.S. forces. Conventional forces began to withdraw, and the last SEAL advisor left Vietnam in March 1973. By 1975, Vietnam fell to the communist forces and became one country again.

The Navy SEALs had fought bravely in the Vietnam War, earning 42 Navy Crosses, 42 Bronze Stars, 2 Legions of Merit, 352 Commendation Medals, and 3 Medals of Honor.

THE GAME ENDS: NAVY SEALS IN THE INVASION OF GRENADA

Operation Urgent Fury was the first major military operation that the Navy SEALs engaged in after the Vietnam War.

In 1974, Grenada gained independence from the United Kingdom. A revolution by the **Marxist** New Jewel Movement suspended the country's constitution and executed the prime minister. Cuba swiftly established ties with Grenada.

UNDERSTAND THE FULL MEANING

Marxist: Committed to the communist philosophy of Karl Marx (1818-1883).

Cuba, a communist country, was a close ally of the Soviet Union. The revolutionary government began to build an airport with assistance from the Soviets. American president Ronald Reagan decided to crush the possibility of another communist dictatorship with military capability in America's backyard. Presidential spokesman Larry Speakers stated about Grenada, "It was a floating craps game down there and we never knew who was in charge," meaning that the government in Grenada was not legitimate or under control.

In 1983, President Ronald Reagan ordered the invasion of Grenada. The Navy SEALs were called upon to perform two missions: Rescue Paul Scoon, a politician under house arrest, and capture Grenada's only radio tower.

The SEAL mission ran into difficulty from the beginning. One of two transport planes missed their **drop zone**, and four SEALs drowned in violently bad weather. Once they entered Grenada, they realized they had forgotten important communications equipment to request backup. They were surrounded by Grenadian and Cuban troops. Using a telephone in the mansion itself, the SEALs called in for backup. They were pinned down in the mansion overnight. Marines came in for backup and rescued the troops along with the governor.

As for the SEALs who entered the radio station, they were able to get inside the station but could not defend their position. They destroyed the station and fought back to water.

UNDERSTAND THE FULL MEANING

drop zone: An area designated for the air delivery of supplies, often behind enemy lines.

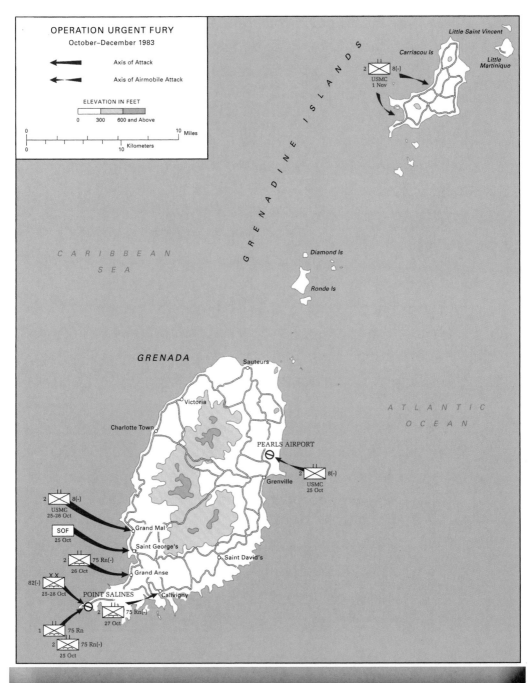

OPERATION URGENT FURY
October–December 1983

Axis of Attack

Axis of Airmobile Attack

ELEVATION IN FEET

0   300   600 and Above

0   10 Miles

0   10 Kilometers

Little Saint Vincent

Carriacou Is

Little Martinique

GRENADINE ISLANDS

2 8(-) USMC 1 Nov

CARIBBEAN SEA

Diamond Is

Ronde Is

ATLANTIC OCEAN

GRENADA

Sauteurs

Victoria

Charlotte Town

PEARLS AIRPORT

Grenville

2 8(-) USMC 25 Oct

2 8(-) USMC 25-28 Oct

SOF 25 Oct

2 75 Rn(-) 26 Oct

Grand Mal

Saint George's

Saint David's

Grand Anse

82(-) 25-28 Oct

POINT SALINES

Calivigny

2 75 Rn(-) 27 Oct

1 75 Rn

2 75 Rn(-) 25 Oct

This map shows the plan of attack for Operation Urgent Fury in Grenada in 1983.

There they hid from patrolling enemy forces. After Grenadian and Cuban forces gave up their search for the Marines, the SEALs swam into the open sea and were rescued by a reconnaissance plane.

It was a brave mission by Special Forces troops. While neither part of their mission went smoothly, they were able to assist the military in crushing the revolutionary government of Grenada.

"I FOUGHT THE LAW AND THE LAW WON": U.S. SEALS IN PANAMA

In 1989, the Navy SEALs performed special operations for the invasion of Panama. During what the military called Operation Just Cause, SEAL teams were ordered to destroy Manuel Noriega's gunboat and private jet. The goal was to stop Noriega from escaping Panama during the invasion of Grenada.

Prior to this invasion, all the missions the Navy SEALs performed since World War II had been top secret. The U.S. government, however, made this SEALs mission public.

Before the invasion began, four Navy SEAL divers swam toward the gunboat while being bombarded by grenades. Two divers descended to the bottom of the Panama Canal, which was beyond the capacity of their breathing units. They destroyed the gunboat with C4 explosives.

UNDERSTAND THE FULL MEANING

reconnaissance: A military mission for the gathering of information about the enemy.

On a separate mission, the SEALs were able to destroy the dictator's plane, but the SEALs lost four men, and thirteen were wounded.

The mission was a success, although it took the lives of many Navy SEALs. Military operations continued against

Flames engulf a building following the outbreak of hostilities between the Panamanian Defense Force and U.S. forces during Operation Just Cause.

SEALs are not only trained to fight in the water. They are prepared for the sort of land warfare they faced in Grenada with training in pistol, rifle, demolitions, and tactical movement.

the Panamanian army for weeks. Forces were closing in on one of the worst Latin American dictators of the Cold War. He took refuge in a building owned by the Vatican (the ruling body of the Roman Catholic church). The military blasted loud rock and roll day and night. Some reports state that the music was used to prevent microphones from eavesdropping on negotiations, but Noriega was also known to hate rock music. Van Halen's song "Panama," as well as the Clash's "I Fought the Law and the Law Won," played over and over. Noriega surrendered in January 1990.

A NEW ERA

From January 1990 to December of 1991, the Soviet Union began to dissolve. The Cold War was over. While Special Forces continued to operate across the world, the United States would not engage in a major war again until after September 11, 2001.

CHAPTER 3

Training and Selection

Just five weeks after the September 11, 2001 attacks, a small handful of Special Forces soldiers landed in Afghanistan and began special operations. On horseback, with the help of other locals, they helped the main branch of the Army topple the Taliban in two months. What the Special Forces achieved required not only technical ability but also language and cultural skills to work with the **counterinsurgency**; the ability to shoot a machine gun was as important as cultural sensitivity.

Not everyone has the opportunity to change history. The military only selects a chosen few to go through training—and then, not everyone passes through training; many are simply not able to take the pressure. For instance, in a part

UNDERSTAND THE FULL MEANING

counterinsurgency: Armed conflict against a rebel force by the officially recognized government.

of military SEAL training known as "hell week," trainees are deprived of sleep and intentionally malnourished for a short amount of time to make sure each recruit is able to work as a team when everything else falls apart.

THE FEW, THE PROUD, THE BRAVE: THE CHALLENGE OF BECOMING A NAVY SEAL

Becoming a Navy SEAL is one of the hardest tasks in the military, which is saying a lot. The motto of the Marines is "the few, the proud, the brave," and the same could be said of a young **cadet**'s experience in the Navy SEAL training program. Harder still is surviving the program. To do this it takes what we call tenacity, the ability to stick to a task, even when it is difficult.

Some common obstacles get in the way. Finding the courage to attempt to even try to become an elite military member is an obstacle in itself. Also, staying in the program is difficult, considering how much training strains the body and mind.

Recruits are carefully chosen; only men with mental and physical **stamina** are able to succeed. The military wants

UNDERSTAND THE FULL MEANING

cadet: A military trainee.

stamina: The ability to withstand physical and mental exertion over a relatively long period of time.

U.S. Navy SEAL students work together to lift Old Misery, a large log used to promote teamwork and unity at the Naval Special Warfare Center at Naval Amphibious Base Coronado.

people who will go on when others give up, who have the high amount of intelligence needed to operate sophisticated tools and weapons. The Navy SEALs have high standards of excellence.

Military recruits look for two main sets of qualities. The first require the same thing needed in all battlefield elites: aggression, physical fitness. and team spirit. The second set

Training

When going through training, the SEALs lose from 70 to 80 percent of their applicants. Ten percent of students don't have the physical ability to make it through training. Another group of people, around 10 to 15 percent of them, will make it through training so long as they are not injured. What is the difference between those who make it and those who don't? Motivation. While all the applicants are considered fit enough to train for Special Forces, you cannot teach attitude as easily as physical fitness. If you come into training with the attitude of a warrior who can overcome any obstacle, you have won half the battle.

of qualities relates to character. Most modern elite units fight in small groups at the forefront of the battle or behind enemy lines. These soldiers need a high degree of self-discipline, motivation, intelligence, and initiative. They must

UNDERSTAND THE FULL MEANING

initiative: The talent for coming up with ideas for dealing with situations and carrying those ideas out.

COST OF TRAINING A SEAL

The Navy SEALs are selective with who they train because training a member of the military to do special missions for the SEALs is expensive and time-consuming. Training a single Navy SEAL can cost up to $500,000. Devoting a large amount of money and time to train a single person comes with risk; the military makes sure it makes the best investment possible.

be dependable and self-reliant in combat. The soldiers must know specialized skills and field tactics.

Training to be in an elite unit in the military requires a great deal of dedication and energy. The military commits time, a lot of money, and energy to training new units. This is why they are very selective about who they train.

Training units will be forced to the limit of their strength. Many train using obstacle courses and even go into situations that simulate being in remote areas. When training, a student will have to do timed runs and sometimes swimming exercises. These physical training exercises will test your body to its limits.

When training for Special Forces you will not only learn normal combat procedures but also special skills. For instance, SEALs will learn anything from demolition to sniping to cracking codes. Training requires intelligence and the ability to learn special skills as much as physical strength. Above all, special operations teach teamwork. Dealing with

U.S. Navy sailor participating in the SEAL Qualification Training (SQT), completes a five-mile hike after finishing the seventh day of close-quarters combat training, at Campo, California.

POLO PLAYERS

In 2010, Navy recruiters funded a study to find what group of people would be most eligible to be a member of the SEALs. The results came in, and water polo players made the top of the list. While this may sound strange at first, the amount of time that water polo players spend in the water and the way the sport uses different parts of the body, as well as their quick reflexes, make water polo players ideal candidates to be Navy SEALs.

physical hardship creates a real bond between the students who stick it out.

The Navy SEALs are one of the hardest organizations to get into and to serve in. Immense amounts of endurance

Loose Ends

If you have any emotional issues with people close to you such as parents or a girlfriend, you should try your best to resolve them before going to camp. Training is stressful enough without having to worry about a problem with a relationship.

and determination are needed to carry out Navy SEAL missions. To apply to the Navy SEALs you must be able to perform a minimum of forty-two push-ups in two minutes. After that, they must do fifty sit-ups in two minutes and be able to perform six pull-ups. A Navy SEAL also must be able to run a mile and a half wearing boots and long pants—in under eleven minutes and thirty seconds.

Up Is Down / Black Is White

When you first enter training, the way things are done may not make complete sense to you; in fact, many things will seem upside down. Try your best not to go into special training with any preconceived ideas about what your lifestyle should be like. Expectations get in the way of experience, and in this case, the ability to adapt to your new circumstances. It is very important to keep a sense of distance from your experience during boot camp. Remind yourself that this experience is only temporary. Maintaining a healthy sense of humor and letting the small stuff go are both highly effective strategies that make boot-camp easier.

Once an applicant has been chosen, the real training begins. The first phase of SEAL training lasts eight weeks. In the first phase, the soldier trains and develops the ability to be comfortable in the water, work as a team, and improve his physical fitness. The physical tasks, which include running, swimming, and calisthenics, become harder as time goes on. Recruits take weekly four-mile timed runs; they go

UNDERSTAND THE FULL MEANING

calisthenics: An organized exercise training program that does not use weights or equipment.

Surfing is what they call it. Lying in the surf as the frigid water rolls over them. It's used to keep the candidates cold and wet—and to weed out the people who don't have the perseverance to continue.

through timed obstacle courses; and they swim long distances. The fourth week of phase one, called "hell week," is the hardest. The military needs to see if a candidate for the

ASVAB

Before you even start trying out for an elite unit, you need to take the ASVAB. The Armed Services Vocational Aptitude Battery is a written test that every military member must take to join the military. It is a timed multi-aptitude test given in over 14,000 schools nationwide. The test is important. Students score in four areas: arithmetic, word knowledge, paragraph comprehension, and mathematics knowledge. The score determines whether or not you can join the military or whether you qualify for a special unit. It also will improve your chances of getting bonuses. Scoring high requires studying, the more the better.

SEALs will crack under pressure. To do this ,they put their trainees through hell week to simulate what a high-stress mission is like.

In the second phase of training, SEAL candidates condition themselves to be combat swimmers. Trainers focus on scuba diving skills. While the trainees learn techniques for diving, they continue extensive physical exercise.

The third phase lasts nine months. This phase trains candidates in the use of weapons and explosives. After the instruction on combat, trainers continue to make physical tasks harder. The running distances become longer. In the final three and a half weeks of training, the trainees apply all the techniques they learned.

The SEALs can be used anywhere the United States needs a special operation. There are units that specialize in working in a specific continent or area in the world. Navy SEALs are prepared at any time military intervention is needed.

If you are interested in joining the Navy SEALs, there is a wealth of information on the Internet. One good source is information.usnavyseals.com. The official website for the SEALs is www.sealswcc.com. Also, you can go to a nearby recruitment office for more specific questions on joining and preparing for the SEALs.

CHAPTER 4
Survival Tactics

The success of a SEAL member can depend as much on stealth and survival as it depends on fierce combat. The sea shows no mercy when it comes to survival; your first mistake in a maritime emergency is likely to be your last. You must master every ocean survival technique in order to live in this unforgiving environment.

Around 71 percent of the Earth's surface is covered by water. It is therefore vital that you learn how to survive in this environment. Human beings' natural place is land, and that makes survival at sea for any length of time difficult. In particular, finding drinking water and food are serious problems for the survivor at sea, though the other dangers the sea poses to the survivor should not be underestimated. The SEALs know how to cope with them all.

First, the SEAL gets to know the environment he faces. The temperature of surface water in the ocean can range from

79° F (26° C) in tropical regions to 29.5° Fahrenheit (–1.4° C), the freezing point of seawater, in polar regions. Around 50 percent of total ocean water has temperatures between 29.5° F (–1.4° C) and 39° F (3.8° C).

But the conditions of the sea vary enormously with the weather. Around the poles in winter, there are violent storms with snow, high winds, and temperatures as low as –122° F (–50° C). Storms in the Atlantic and Pacific oceans can result in waves higher than a three-story house. In contrast, in some areas of the Atlantic, Pacific, and Indian oceans, there are times and places where there are no surface winds at all. The sea in these conditions becomes incredibly still, with no wind to help you travel if your boat does not have a motor.

Waterspouts (the equivalent of tornadoes at sea) are common off the Atlantic and Gulf coasts and along the coasts of China and Japan. Hurricanes and typhoons occur in the warm areas of all the oceans during the summer and fall. They can last up to two weeks.

READING THE WEATHER

Sailors and SEALs are very aware of signs that indicate which way the weather is likely to turn. Two good indicators are the wind and the clouds. By recognizing the direction and changes of wind, the types of cloud, and the likely weather they indicate, you can prepare better for either good or bad weather. In the summer in particular, the land is warmer

An HH-60H Seahawk helicopter lifts two SEAL swimmers from the water off the coast of Oahu, Hawaii following a rendezvous with the nuclear-powered submarine USS Kamehameha during special operations training.

Understanding clouds and other weather information is vital for SEALs when they are parachuting into a region.

than the sea during the day, but it is colder than the sea at night.

Clouds can be incredibly useful for surviving at sea because they can tell you a lot about what type of weather is heading your way. There are four main groups of clouds, categorized by the cloud's height above the Earth: cirrus, cumulus, nimbus, and stratus.

Usually about 4 miles (6 km) above the Earth, cirrus clouds are composed of ice particles. They are feathery and long, and they look like streaky bands. They are known as mare's tails. These clouds can often indicate fine weather, but when they are accompanied by a north wind in cold climates, they sometimes precede a blizzard. Within the cirrus category are cirrostratus and cirrocumulus. Cirrostratus consists of a fine veil of whitish clouds, darker than cirrus. When cirrostratus follows cirrus across the sky, bad weather may be about to arrive, so now is the time to make preparations. Cirrocumulus clouds give a different message. These clouds are small white balls arranged in groups, and they indicate good weather.

Fluffy, white, and heaped together, cumulus clouds are often indicators of fine weather. They can appear around midday on a sunny day. If they pile up and push higher into the atmosphere, they can become storm clouds.

Nimbus clouds paint the whole sky a uniform gray color. This can mean bad weather, but it is even more serious if you see cumulonimbus. Towering into the atmosphere, these clouds are anvil shape at the top, looking like cirrus. They often mean sudden heavy showers of rain, snow, or hail. If a thunderstorm occurs, you can expect a strong wind from the direction of the storm, as well as a rapid drop in temperature.

The final category, stratus, consists of low clouds composed of water droplets that make up an even, gray layer of cloud. They inevitably mean rain or snow. Within stratus is altostratus. Holes in this layer mean that the weather may not be too bad. Finally, comes nimbostratus. These rain-bearing clouds have a low base and consist of thick layers.

The clouds can tell you what the weather will be like, but you also need to be able to read the winds. SEALs always need to know what weather is heading their way for their missions.

SWIMMING AND SURVIVAL

Being thrown into the sea can literally take your breath away. The SEALs teach you that in these situations there is no substitute for a clear and calm mind that helps you work out how to survive.

In survival circumstances, SEALs know it is better to keep your clothing on when in the water. If abandoning a ship or aircraft, take whatever warm clothing is available as well as easily portable food (chocolate and candies). Do not jump into the water with an inflated life jacket, because the impact may be dangerous.

Once in the water, inflate your life jacket, swim steadily, and look for any floating objects, such as pieces of wood that will help you keep afloat. Use a lift raft if you have one.

U.S. Navy sailors enrolled in the basic underwater demolition/SEAL course approach the shore during an over-the-beach exercise at San Clemente Island, California. The exercise is designed to prepare SEAL's for missions that begin in the water before transitioning to land.

U.S. Naval sea cadets build up their teamwork at the end of their swim by squatting in unison and performing various exercises as instructed by their operations instructor. The course not only educates the sea cadets about Naval Special Warfare community but also emphasizes teamwork and individual accomplishment in the team environment.

If you escape from a downed aircraft, swim or paddle upwind, especially if the plane is on fire. Remember, any large object, such as a plane or boat, will create suction when it sinks beneath the surface and can drag survivors down with it. Therefore, get away from the plane or boat as soon as possible.

If there is burning oil on the water, try to swim under it, using an underwater breaststroke. You may need to deflate or throw away your life jacket for this. When you need to come up for air, leave enough time to clear a space in the burning area by pushing the water aside from beneath the surface. Then take in enough breath, and if possible, look to check the shortest route to clear water before submerging again, straight downward, feet first.

Once clear of immediate danger, practice relaxing by floating on your back with your face above the water. This will let you gather your energy before swimming again to the nearest life raft or large floating object. If no life raft is available, but you are wearing a life jacket, adopt the Heat Escaping Lessing Posture (HELP) to keep as much body warmth as possible. The principle of HELP is keeping the head clear of the water, since most heat is lost through the head and neck.

If you have nothing to help you stay afloat, you can save energy by relaxing into a crouching position, which will let your body float just below the surface of the water, and then move your arms to bring your head up to the surface to breathe before relaxing into the crouch position again. However, these measures are only temporary—you must get out of the water. If you do not, you could quickly freeze to death in cold water.

If you are lucky, you might have found your way into a life raft. When in a raft, the SEALs immediate priorities are rescue, protection from the elements, and water to drink. Obey the following rules:

- Give first aid to any wounded survivors.

- Check that any signaling equipment is ready to use. This may include flares, emergency radio, and flags. Save batteries of signaling equipment by using them only when search aircraft or ships are in range.

- Salvage any useful material that may be floating nearby. (It can be tied to the dinghy—if you have one—to provide more space inside.)

- Ensure that one member of the crew is attached to the lift raft with a line in case it tips over and is blown away.

- If you have a supply of drinking water, do not drink it all at once—ration it out.

- Check available supplies of food.

Follow the survival instructions you find on the life raft. Remove wet clothing when you can, and dry it out. In a cold climate, huddle together to share warmth. In a hot climate, keep at least one layer of clothing on to protect the body from the direct powerful light and heat of the sun. If any survivors have dry clothes, they should share them with those who are wet. Those who are wet should be given the most sheltered positions in the raft, and they should be allowed to warm their hands and feet against those who are dry. If possible, give extra water rations to those suffering from cold exposure. You should exercise fingers, toes, legs, arms, shoulders, and buttocks to help keep you fit and strong. In a sitting position, put your hands under your armpits and raise your feet slightly off the ground. Keep them up for a minute or two. Try to exercise at least twice a day.

These actions should help you survive. But your goal is to be seen or to find safety. Your chances of being found are

SEAL Qualification Training students ride an inflatable boat in San Diego Bay during the twelve-day maritime operations segment of their training program. Students are trained to operate from fixed-wing aircraft, helicopters, Navy surface ships, submarines, and combatant-craft.

greatest if you are close to the area where rescuers were last in radio contact. Stay in the area for at least 72 hours to give them a chance to find you.

The following actions will help your chances of being rescued:

- Put out a sea anchor in order to stay close to the site. When open, the anchor will help to keep the raft in one place. When closed, it will cause the life raft to be pulled along by the current.

- Signaling and navigation equipment should be carefully protected from the elements, but have them ready to use quickly.

- Exercise leadership skills where necessary and give people tasks to do (such as being a signaler, navigator, spotter, and fisherman). Try to find out who has any specialized skills that might be useful.

- If you are not the leader, concentrate on carrying out your particular job effectively as best you can. Do not interfere with other people's skills unless asked.

- You will be thinking most clearly in the early stages of survival when you are reasonably well fed and watered, so make plans then you can remember and follow if things become difficult and you become weaker.

- Put up any permanent signals, such as a flag.

- Keep a log, recording the prevailing winds, weather, currents, and state of the crew on board. This will help in such matters as navigation.

Members of the SEALs from Golf Platoon conduct an exercise in a combat rubber raiding craft.

If rescue has not come or if, for some reason, you consider this to be unlikely (it may be that no one knows you
are there), then the SEALs say you should try to find land.
Several signs may tell you if land is nearby:

- A stationary cumulus cloud can mean an island.
- Birds will often be heading toward land in the after-
  noon and evening. Look out for the particular types
  of bird and the direction in which they are flying. If it
  is the morning, they will most likely be heading away
  from land.
- A lagoon can create a greenish reflection on the
  underside of clouds.
- Floating vegetation and pieces of timber may indicate
  the proximity of land.
- Water that is muddy with silt has probably come from
  the mouth of a large river that is nearby.
- Deep water is dark green or dark blue; a lighter color
  indicates shallow water and perhaps land.

Once you have sighted land, your goal is to reach it as soon
as possible. If you are swimming, wear your shoes and at
least one thickness of clothing. Use the side or breaststroke
to save your strength. Water is calmer in the sheltered side
of a heavy growth of seaweed. Do not swim through it; crawl
over the top, grasping the vegetation. Swimming ashore can
be difficult because of sea currents and hidden rocks. Ride

in on the back of a small wave, swimming forward with it. In high waves, swim toward the shore in the trough between waves. Put your face down and submerge yourself beneath the waves, then swim forward in the next trough. If caught beneath a large wave, let it pass over you, and then push off the bottom with your feet, or swim if in deep water. When landing on a rocky shore, aim for the place where the waves rush up onto the rocks, not where they explode with a high white spray. To land, advance behind a large wave into the breakers. Face the shore with your feet in front, two to three feet lower than your head. In this way, your feet will absorb shocks when you land or hit submerged rocks or reefs, and you will not get injured.

If you do not reach shore behind the wave you have selected, swim using your hands only. Adopt a sitting position as the next wave approaches and carries you to shore. Once ashore, you will need other survival skills. But whether you are on land or at sea, in order to survive you need to know where you are going.

FINDING FOOD AND WATER

You are surrounded by water at sea—and unfortunately, none of it is drinkable. You must find ways to provide yourself with food and drinking water or you might not survive for more than a few days.

At sea, water is your most precious commodity, as any Navy SEAL will tell you. Do not be tempted to use sea water for drinking or for mixing with fresh water. It is likely to cause vomiting and serious illness. The minimum requirement of fresh drinking water is one pint (475 ml) a day. Follow these ration rules strictly to increase your chances of survival:

- Day 1: Give no water. The body can make use of its own water reserves. Be strict with this rule.

- Days 2–4: Give 14 fluid ounces (400 ml) if available.

- Day 5 onward: Give two to eight fluid ounces (55–225 ml) daily, depending on water availability and climate.

If you have no way of measuring the fluid, devise a ration that will give you all a supply of water for over a week, and do not drink for the first 24 hours, or until you have a headache. A big problem is that you lose your body's water through sweating. Follow these SEAL guidelines strictly for reducing your use of body water. In hot climates, reduce sweating by staying still and saving your energy. Brush dried salt off your body with a dry cloth. Try to sleep and rest as much as possible. Try not to get seasick, since vomiting causes you to lose valuable fluids. Relax and focus your mind on other tasks. Suck on a button to make saliva and reduce your desire to drink. In a hot climate, keep out of direct sunlight and dampen clothes during the day to keep cool, but do not get overwet or get water in the raft. If there is not enough water, do not eat, because the food will absorb water from your body. In a hot climate, in particular, food is secondary to water. Watch out for rain and make sure you catch it in a tarpaulin or containers. Store as much as possible and

SEALs prepare for many kinds of emergencies at sea. Here, special warfare combatant-craft crewmen learn the procedure for getting out of a parachute harness when entangled by two parachutes underwater.

always sip water in a slow, steady way to avoid vomiting. Let the body absorb the water rather than overfilling your stomach. Moisten your lips and mouth before swallowing.

Apart from rain, there are other ways of finding water. One is a **solar still**. A life raft may be supplied with a solar still. Read the instructions carefully because the still will not work unless the sea is relatively calm. You can also make a solar still by placing a plastic sheet over a container and securing it with whatever is on hand. Place coins or a stone in the center of the sheet. In the morning, the sun raises the overall temperature of the air to produce vapor. Water then condenses on the underside of the sheet and runs down into the container.

Icebergs provide a source of water in cold climates. Old sea ice will have lost much of its saltiness, but new ice will taste unpleasant. You can recognize old ice by its smooth shapes and blue color. Do not approach large or moving icebergs, since these may crush the life raft or overturn it suddenly.

It is advisable to eat nothing for as long as possible and remember not to eat too much if little water is available. However, food will be essential if you are to survive for a few days. When it comes to finding food, fish are the obvious choice for SEALs. Fish will be your main food source. Flying fish may even jump into your raft! In the open sea, without land in sight, fish are generally safe to eat. However, do not eat fish that are brightly colored, covered with bristles or

UNDERSTAND THE FULL MEANING

solar still: A tool used to clean water and make it drinkable.

Learning to survive heavy surf conditions is one of the most physically demanding aspects of becoming a Navy SEAL.

spines, or those that puff up or have parrot-like mouths or teeth like humans. Also, avoid fish eggs in clusters or clumps; these will be poisonous.

Catching fish is not easy if you are **improvising**, but the SEALs are expert fishermen as well as expert soldiers. Follow their advice for safe fishing:

- Do not touch the fishing line with your bare hand when reeling in, and never wrap it around your hands or tie it in an inflatable dinghy. The salt on it makes a sharp cutting edge that is a danger to your hands and the raft.

- If you have gloves, wear them when handling fish; that way, you will not get fins or fish teeth in your skin.

- Pass a net under your raft from one end to the other, since fish and turtles are attracted to the shade under your raft. (You need at least two people to perform this.)

- Use a flashlight to attract fish at night.

- Make improvised hooks from small pieces of wire and small bright objects.

Use the guts of a fish, or organ meats, that you have caught previously or a small fish as bait to catch larger fish (though they can also be used as food). Cut loose fish

UNDERSTAND THE FULL MEANING

improvising: Coming up with new strategies as situations develop and change; often learning as you go along.

that are too large to handle, and do not fish if sharks may be near. Head for large groups of fish, but remember that shark and barracuda may also be present. Be careful not to puncture the dinghy with fishhooks. You can also bind a knife to an oar to use as a spear to catch fish.

Experiment with different ways of fishing and find out what works best for you. Once you have caught a fish, you should gut it immediately. This is not pleasant, but it has to be done. Slit the fish with your knife from the anus to just behind the gills, and pull out the internal organs. Clean the flesh, then cut off the fins and tail. Cut down to but not through the spine. Cut around the spine, finishing behind the gills on both sides. Insert your thumb along the top of the spine and begin to pull it away from the flesh. The ribs should come out cleanly with the spine. Eat the fish raw.

Fish are not all you can eat at sea. All seabirds are edible, for example, and they will be attracted to your raft as a perching place. Wait until they land on your raft, then try to grab them before they fly away. However, the best method is to use a hook covered in fish, which can be trailed behind the boat. The hook gets stuck in seabirds' throat. Use a noose or net, similarly camouflaged, to trap their legs.

Some seaweed can also be eaten, but only if they are firm to the touch and odorless. Do not eat slender, branched varieties of seaweed, since these contain acids that will make you feel ill. Make sure no sea creatures are attached to the seaweed before eating it. You can collect seaweed around shorelines and in mid-ocean. Remember that seaweed absorbs fluids when your body is digesting it, so it should not be eaten when water is scarce. You should eat only small amounts of seaweed at a time, because it can cause you to have bowel movements or need to urinate, losing more precious water from your body.

Not everything the SEALs do is a life-or-death situation! Here they are using their skills in the water to help clean trash and debris out of the ocean.

If fish, birds, and seaweed are not enough for survival, then a SEAL will also eat plankton. Plankton consists of tiny plants and animals that drift around or swim weakly in the oceans. They can be caught by dragging a net through the water. Plankton contains many nutrients, yet it can make you ill when eaten in large quantities. If you are living solely on plankton, therefore, you must eat small quantities at first. In addition, you should ensure you have an adequate supply of drinking water; digesting plankton will use up your body fluids. Each plankton catch should be thoroughly checked before you eat it: remove all jellyfish tentacles (be careful not to get stung), discard the plankton that have become jelly-like, and check for species that are spiny. If the catch contains large amounts of spiny plankton, you can dry or crush it before eating.

SURVIVING ON LAND, STAYING HIDDEN

It is vital that an elite soldier knows where he is at all times behind enemy lines. If soldiers get lost, then they are more likely to be discovered, and their mission is more likely to fail. An important aspect of navigation is called "terrain analysis." This means looking at the ground in front of you, then looking at the map, and seeing if there any differences between the two. Terrain analysis involves things like working out which way the rivers run, which features can be seen at night, and the position of fences and other man-made

SEALs must be able to navigate on land as well, including in thickly wooded forest or jungle regions.

features. In terrain such as dense jungle, where the only thing to be seen is trees, elite soldiers will have to use their compasses to navigate, which will mean literally holding them in front of them. At night, the military compasses are luminous (glow in the dark), so that they can still be seen.

Another method of navigating is called "dead reckoning." Dead reckoning means that soldiers plot their journey before they set out on a mission, and plan it in a series of stages. Each one is measured in terms of distance and direction between two points. These courses lead them from the starting point to the final destination. They help the soldiers to find out where they are at any one time, either by following their plan or comparing where they are on the ground to where they are on the map.

Once they have worked out where they are going and plotted their route on a map, elite soldiers will mark out route cards. These describe each stage of the route they intend to travel. When SEALs have completed their route cards, they are ready to move. When moving, they must keep track of the direction they are heading and the distance they have covered. If they deviate from their route, they must make adjustments to the route cards and their map-reading. However, if they are operating in an area where contact with the enemy is likely, they will not write anything down, because this information may be useful to an enemy if they are captured.

Knowing as much as possible about the enemy will help an elite team find out valuable military information. This involves knowing where the enemy is and what he is doing, and this must be done by tracking. A careless enemy will leave telltale signs of his presence, which can then be used against him. Moved stones, crumbled stones pressed into the earth, or bent grasses are signs that an enemy patrol has been in the area. Stains are another sign. These may include blood, water on stones, and crushed leaves.

Garbage indicates the presence of ill-disciplined soldiers, though booby traps may have been left among the garbage to kill the unwary. Sounds can also tell the unit where the enemy is. Soldiers can place their ears on the ground or on a stick driven six inches (15 cm) into the ground. It is hard to work out the direction of the noises, but sounds can be heard from a long distance because the ground actually carries noise better than the air. Sounds will carry farther in light mist, though rain or wind can mask them. Rain may also cause soldiers to miss sounds if they are wearing hoods or caps; it can be worth having a wet head in order to hear sounds. During a night operation, no one should wear a hat or helmet. Helmets make hollow sounds in the rain, whistle during breezes, and generally rattle and rustle.

Poor enemy camouflage can also be a signpost to an attacking team. In particular, team members should look for straight lines (rarely found in nature), unusual differences in color or tone, and unnatural vegetation, such as green leaves among dead branches. Having detected the enemy, a team must work out their distance to them. This can be difficult. Judging distances depends on a soldier's skill and the amounts of water vapor in the air. Clear, desert air, for example, helps a soldier to detect sights at a greater dis-

A group of Navy SEALs prepares to cross Phelan Creek during Northern Edge 2009. Northern Edge is a joint exercise focusing on detecting and tracking units at sea, in the air, and on land. The Northern Warfare Training Center and the SEALs worked together on river crossing techniques and rope handling.

tance, but does not carry sound or odors as well as more humid air. Sounds can be a real problem when estimating distances, since they can bounce among buildings and rocky terrain and mislead you as to the direction of their source. Sound travels at around 1,000 feet (300 m) per second, so the elite soldier should count the seconds between seeing the flash of a weapon firing and hearing its bang. The number of seconds multiplied by 1,000 equates to the distance to the weapon in feet.

BEING INVISIBLE

Even if elite soldiers are master shots with their rifles, or experts at blowing up bridges, they must still learn how to become virtually invisible while doing all these things. This is the art of hiding. Elite soldiers who are behind enemy lines cannot do anything useful if detected. The three essential techniques of remaining unseen are known as cover, concealment, and camouflage.

Concealment is the art of stopping yourself from being seen. It may be natural concealment—such as bushes, grass, and shadows—or artificial, with the soldier using materials such as camouflage nets. Successful concealment, both natural and artificial, may depend on the season, weather, and light.

Soldiers use camouflage to mask the color, outline, or texture of themselves and their equipment. Vegetation or other materials that grow in the area provide natural—and the best—camouflage. When looked at closely, man-made

Members of a West Coast-based Navy SEAL team participate in infiltration and exfiltration training during a Northern Edge 2009 training exercise. An Army aviation unit transported the SEALS in CH-47D Chinook helicopters, performing two-wheel landings atop mountainous terrain in the Joint Pacific Alaska Range Complex. The SEAL team wears camouflage to make themselves "invisible" during infiltration.

substances will always appear to be man-made. The secret of camouflage is to never draw the attention of the enemy or create a reason for the enemy to investigate your position.

Many things can give you away. These include cut branches when you are building a concealed shelter (known as a hide); poorly concealed hide edges; equipment left outside the hide; and, of course, garbage left outside the hide. A soldier needs to remember than the enemy can smell, too: food should be eaten without cooking if possible. Maintaining stealth and being quiet is important. A soldier should walk as quietly as possible. Anything that might rattle should be taped down to keep it quiet. Team members should send messages through hand signals. Because sound carries best at night, noise of any kind should be reduced to zero.

When communicating, do not imitate birdcalls. Unless your enemy is stupid, they will know these signals are not birds chirping. Most birds call in the early morning and evening. They do not call to each other in the middle of the night. Owls hoot, but how many owls do you hear? Are they native to the area? Owls stick to one area their entire lives. If the enemy has been in an area for several weeks without hearing an owl, and then hears two owls hooting back and forth, the special unit's cover will be blown. Any noise you make will be assumed a threat.

The "Five Ss"—shape, shine, shadow, silhouette, and spacing—are important to remember when using camouflage. When camouflaging yourself, make sure that you avoid these five things. Straight lines, always a sign of human presence, should be avoided. Cover rifle barrels with bits of cam-

These SEALs are preparing for a training exercise in infiltration of a wooded area. They are wearing camouflage designed for this region, and their faces are painted. They wear net gloves for ease of movement while still disguising their hands' color.

ouflaged material. Anything reflective or bright should be made dull, from the face (camouflaged with greasepaint) to the heels of boots. Anything smooth should be made rough or crinkly. Movement should be within shadows wherever possible, and creating shadows, even on the body, should be avoided. Keep away from crests and skylines that might make you stand in silhouette.

Soldiers have to be prepared to move slowly to their objective. The enemy (or, for trainee soldiers, the instructors) will notice not only human movement but sudden flights (and the alarm calls) of birds of animals, odd movements of plants and bushes, and so on. Camouflage has to be the right color and may have to be changed frequently so that the soldier constantly blends into the background. Grass and saplings grow up toward the sun, so a patch of strangely flattened vegetation will instantly raise suspicion.

The best hope a soldier has of remaining invisible when moving in grass and woodland is the "ghillie suit," an outfit made up of hundreds of strips of camouflaged cloth. The soldier wearing this suit may look like a scarecrow, but the camouflage is excellent. The suit, which can take up to 50 hours to make, was created by gamekeepers (ghillies) in the Scottish Highlands in the nineteenth century. A ghillie suit is hot and heavy. But surviving on the battlefield has never been comfortable.

In cities, various shades of gray seem to make the most effective camouflage, and here the occasional straight line and smooth surface will blend into the man-made background. White suits, usually looser than standard uniform to break up the human profile, are worn against full snow or ice. Where there is ground snow but none on the trees, wearing a woodland camouflage jacket and white pants is best. In the desert, a ghillie suit should not be worn. Desert environments are the most difficult places for camouflage. Using sand-colored uniforms in the camouflage suit pattern, along with whatever local vegetation there is (if any), are the soldier's best hopes.

When on a reconnaissance mission, one of the best ways to stay hidden is by building a camouflaged shelter, a "hide." What kind of shelter the soldier builds depends on the mission. A soldier may simply build an arrangement of bushes and grasses to hide for a few minutes. A long **surveillance** mission can involve building a complex shelter with a roof and observation holes to view the enemy through. The front of such a hide should be made bulletproof, often by heaping up a bank of soil and stone in front of it. The shelter should be big enough to the give the team some movement; this will help them exercise stiff muscles. Perhaps most important, the hide should not be set up in a position that would be obviously used for reconnaissance. The enemy will likely be watching for obvious spots like the tops of hills.

If soldiers follow these techniques, they should be able to operate behind enemy lines without being discovered. It takes nerves of steel to survive surrounded by the enemy, but the world's elite forces are trained to do just that.

UNDERSTAND THE FULL MEANING

surveillance: Close observation.

CHAPTER 5
Modern Missions Around the World

Today the Navy SEALs perform a wide variety of tasks. Currently, the SEALs participate in special missions for the two wars in which America is engaged, in Afghanistan and Iraq. At times, SEAL teams are also needed to protect American interests abroad when those interests are compromised by military threats. The SEALs also participate in humanitarian missions, helping those who are in need of assistance from the U.S. government.

PROTECTING TRADE ABROAD

Protecting U.S. commercial interests abroad is one of the major functions of SEAL Special Forces. Currently, more and more goods travel across the world. Naturally, there are illegal forces that sometimes get in the way, especially when money is involved. In some cases, the United Sates sends the SEALs on special missions to protect the security of the open seas. These conflicts are not always against nation-states.

PIRATES!

The SEALs perform military operations outside of conventional warfare. In 2010, President Barack Obama called upon the Navy SEALs and Marines to rescue an American hostage from Somali pirates.

Pirating has come back as a serious danger for many around the "Horn of Africa" region, which is in the easternmost part of Africa. It is the southern part of the Somali Peninsula. More than 120 pirate attacks occurred near this area in 2008. Somali pirates have stolen more than 100 million dollars from various illegal activities around the area. One of the most profitable ways of making money is to hold for ransom important passengers of the ships they board. One of the Somali pirates' greatest successes was taking a Ukrainian freighter packed with tanks, antiaircraft guns, and other weapons. After four months, the Ukrainian government paid over three million dollars to get the ship back. This was not an unusual occurrence; it was the twenty-sixth attack in the area in 2008. What was unusual was the effectiveness of the pirates in getting what they wanted.

But they didn't get what they wanted when they took Captain Richard Phillips hostage in April 2010. After the pirates repeatedly threatened to kill the captain if the U.S. government did not pay money, President Obama authorized the Marines and Navy to use force if necessary.

It was a standoff. Then the pirates began to run out of food, water, and fuel. Eventually one of the pirates surrendered because of an injured hand. Another dramatic moment occurred when Captain Phillips tried to escape by jumping out of a lifeboat on April 10th, but the pirates recaptured him.

On the evening of April 12th, two of Phillips' captors poked their heads out of the lifeboat; the third was visible from a window in the bow. He was pointing an automatic rifle at Captain Phillips. It was the perfect opportunity for American snipers who were watching.

THE SEALS AT WAR

Wherever the United States fights battles against countries that threaten our security, the SEALs can be counted on to support the Army in special missions. When the World Trade Towers were struck down, the United States invaded Afghanistan. The Taliban government protected Al Qaeda and allowed them to train terrorists who committed attacks abroad. The cost of occupying Afghanistan would not come cheap. All knew that the lives of young men in the military would be lost. President Bush stated in a speech soon after the war in Afghanistan began:

In the months ahead, our patience will be one of our strengths . . . patience in all the sacrifices that may

Trust Your Instincts

A lieutenant walks down an empty road in Ramadi, Iraq; he sees an object in the road that obviously looks like one of the homemade bombs that litter Iraq. As they bring out the equipment, they find that the bomb was a decoy, a fake bomb to distract American troops. One of their troops states that a concrete object in the middle of a pile of rubble ahead looked "too symmetrical . . . too perfect." The lieutenant has the area cleared and found that there was a bomb encased in concrete.

Army researcher Steven Burnett did a study involving perception and emotional responses. He found that listening to your emotions could help you detect real dangers. Navy SEALs have the capacity to control their emotions, but they should still listen to them. Burnett says, "Not long ago people thought of emotions as old stuff, as just feelings—feelings that had little to do with rational decision . . . or got in the way of it . . . now that position

come. Today, those sacrifices are being made by members of our armed forces who now defend us so far from home, and by their proud and worried families.

Operation Red Wings in Afghanistan is a reminder of the necessary cost of waging war: the loss of our Special Forces' lives.

has reversed. We understand emotions . . . work to solve a problem, often before we're conscious of it."

Studies of the NAVY SEALs and Green Berets found that the stress hormone, cortisol, rushes through their minds just like anyone else. However, their levels of cortisol drop faster than less-trained troops. In other words, Special Forces units experience the same emotions as anyone else; they have just learned to manage them better.

A superhero with X-ray vision could not pick up most IEDs, but veterans state that they can pick up subtle, nearly unconscious danger signals: a faint feeling of tension in the air, Iraqi villagers acting slightly different, an odd inflection in an Afghani voice. These are signals that may release stress hormones before we can put what is wrong into exact words.

If you get a swelling of fear when you approach a situation, your mind could be detecting threats that your conscious mind cannot pick up. Trust your instincts.

SEALS IN AFGHANISTAN: OPERATION RED WINGS

Michael P. Murphy graduated from Penn State and was accepted at several law schools. Instead, he decided to join the U.S. Navy SEAL Team. He had a promising military career, a fiancée at home, and loving parents.

In 2005, Michael and three other Navy SEALs were assigned to complete Operation Red Wings. They were

deployed there to gather information and kill Taliban leader Ahmad Shah, a terrorist who had grown up near the area and now commanded the "Mountain Tigers," a group of insurgents. While the SEALs were at first able to **infiltrate** the mountain-filled area, they were detected in their hiding place by a group of local goat herders. There was an argument between the four SEALs about what to do with the group of men who had stumbled on them.

Navy SEALs operating in Afghanistan in support of Operation Enduring Freedom. From left to right, Sonar Technician (Surface) 2nd Class Matthew G. Axelson, Senior Chief Information Systems Technician Daniel R. Healy, Quartermaster 2nd Class James Suh, Hospital Corpsman 2nd Class Marcus Luttrell, Machinist's Mate 2nd Class Eric S. Patton, and Lt. Michael P. Murphy. With the exception of Luttrell, all were killed June 28, 2005, by enemy forces while supporting Operation Red Wing.

They had to make a decision. One SEAL voted to kill the villagers, one voted to release then, and one did not want to vote. This meant it was up to a man named Luttrell. Luttrell voted to set the villagers free. He told the *Washington Post*

Profile of a Hero: Michael A. Monsoor

Michael Monsoor was a Navy SEAL operating with a group of Iraqi snipers who were positioned on a roof-top in an area heavy with insurgents in Ar Ramadi, Iraq. They were there to detect enemy movement quickly, so they could be the first to attack. The insurgents discovered Monsoor's reconnaissance team and surrounded them on the morning of September 29, 2006. At first, Iraqi snipers were able to take down two insurgents. The rebel forces continued to attack the team, assaulting them with rocket-propelled grenade and gunfire. An insurgent threw a grenade at the American forces. It landed directly in front of Monsoor. Without hesitation, he gave his life for his team, throwing himself onto the grenade to buffer the blast. He received a posthumous Medal of Honor.

later, "The military guy in me wanted to kill them," but "they just seemed like—people. I'm not a murderer."

Whether or not it was the villagers themselves that alerted the Taliban of the soldier's presence is not known. Regardless, the decision still haunts Luttrell. A large group of insurgents

UNDERSTAND THE FULL MEANING

deployed: Military personnel moved into a combat zone.

infiltrate: To secretly pass troops through enemy lines.

A Navy SEAL team member provides security from a rooftop as part of a non-combatant evacuation exercise during Desert Rescue XI at a naval air station. The exercise simulates the rescue of downed aircrew behind enemy lines, enabling other aircrews to perform combat search-and-rescue missions as well as experiment with new techniques in realistic scenarios.

later surrounded and attacked the group. All four of the SEALs suffered wounds during the intense gunfire. They began to leap down the mountainside, trying to find a clear area to get help. Forty-five minutes into the struggle, the communications officer of the group attempted to get out of the mountainous area to call back to their base. Taliban leaders shot him in the hand, shattering his thumb.

Murphy knew they had to call out for help for at least part of his team to survive. Murphy realized he had to take a risk; without requesting assistance, all four of them would not survive. So, without any regard for his own safety he bounded off the mountainside, exposing himself to enemy gunfire. He was shot while trying to communicate for backup, but he continued trying to get through. In his final moments of life, he returned fire against the enemy. Before he died, Murphy achieved his goal: he made contact.

But the battle was not over. The remaining SEAL team continued fighting over hills and cliffs. When the rescue forces came, a rocket-propelled grenade shot down the helicopter. All sixteen of the passengers on the helicopter died: eight SEALs and eight Army Special Forces units. Luttrell was able to escape, walking and crawling seven miles. While he escaped, he shot six more Taliban fighters. After wandering the mountains for several days, he found Sabri-Minah, a Pashtun village. The villagers there sheltered Lieutenant Luttrell. The Taliban demanded they hand the wounded SEAL over and even offered to bribe them, but they refused. Later, a village elder walked 20 miles to the nearest Army base. Luttrell was finally rescued, six days after the battle.

Operation Red Wings saw the worst loss of life for the U.S. Military since the invasion of Afghanistan. It was also the largest loss for the SEALs since World War II.

All three members of Murphy's team were awarded the Navy Cross, making their team the most **decorated** team in the history of the Navy SEALs.

PEACEFUL WARRIORS: HUMANITARIAN MISSIONS

The Navy SEALs are not only called to protect American interests with their weapons. At times, protecting America means helping nations that need assistance. In times of hardship, the SEALs can be counted on to help those who suffer from disasters.

A BIG BOOST: HUMANITARIAN MISSION IN THE PHILIPPINES

The Philippine government and the United States have been allies for a long time. The U.S. Military trained Philippine troops in the past, but in 2009, the Philippines needed a different form of help from the Navy SEALs.

After Typhoon Ketsana flooded the Philippine Islands, many were affected by the massive amount of flooding that swept through the nation; the typhoon hit Manila especially

UNDERSTAND THE FULL MEANING

decorated: Having received military honors, especially medals.

Painting an elementary school building after a typhoon may not seem as exciting work as some of the other Navy SEAL missions, but team members took pride in helping Manila get back on its feet after the natural disaster.

James Woods, a retired Navy SEAL assigned to the U.S. Navy Parachute Team, the Leap Frogs, shows students how to pack his parachute after the Team gave a parachute demonstration at Brooke High School. The Leap Frogs are based in San Diego and perform at various locations across the country to showcase Navy excellence and raise awareness about Naval Special Warfare.

hard. Hundreds of thousands of people lost their homes due to the flood.

Navy SEALs provided support to affected towns. They rescued residents of towns and villages devastated by the typhoon. The SEALs transported displaced Filipinos to churches and schools. Teams also delivered food and fresh water where it was needed.

A Filipino congressman stated, "The work the U.S. Military did was terrific. . . . I was very thankful for U.S. support. Your teams were able to successfully go to Santa Lucia High School to help deliver food. It was a big boost that your people were helping us out."

CAREERS AFTER THE MILITARY

There is a whole world of opportunity after a soldier finishes being a Navy SEAL. The paths SEALs choose after they are done serving their country are as different as the gentlemen who answer the call of duty.

After serving in Afghanistan as a pilot and mission commander of a two-man submarine, Christopher Cassidy went on to join NASA in 2004. By 2006, he had completed Astronaut Candidate Training, which is quite extensive, involving flight training, space training, and scientific training. He has already performed three spacewalks to help install components of a Japanese space station.

Richard Marcinko led an assault in Vietnam that was so successful the Navy referred to it as "the most successful SEAL operation in the Mekong River's Delta." He was awarded a total of four Bronze stars throughout his military career. Marcinko has a long list of activities he's engaged in since retiring from the Navy SEALs. He pursued a career as an author and co-produced a video game. His autobiography, *Rogue Warrior*, was a *New York Times* best seller. He has followed *Rogue Warrior* up with sequels. And, last but not least, he is a conservative political commentator and has done consulting work for Fox Channel's television show, 24.

Navy SEALs know how to take the best in life and apply the courage they learned on the battlefield to civilian life.

FIND OUT MORE ON THE INTERNET

Air Force www.airforce.com

Army Recruiting www.goarmy.com

Department of Defense www.defense.gov

Marine Corps www.marines.com

Navy www.navy.com

U.S. Naval Academy www.usna.edu

West Point www.usma.edu

The websites listed on this page were active at the time of publication. The publisher is not responsible for websites that have changed their address or discontinued operation since the date of publication. The publisher will review and update the websites upon each reprint.

FURTHER READING

Banmanyar, Mir, with Chris Osman. *SEALs: The US Navy's Elite Fighting Force.* Oxford, UK: Osprey Publishing, 2008.

Couch, Dick. *Down Range: Navy SEALs in the War on Terrorism.* New York: Three Rivers Press, 2006.

——. *The Finishing School: Earning the Navy SEAL Trident.* New York: Three Rivers Press, 2005.

Flach, Andrew. *The Official United States Navy SEAL Workout.* Long Island City, N.Y.: Hatherleigh, 2002.

Pfarrer, Chuck. *Warrior Soul: The Memoir of a Navy SEAL.* New York: Presidio Press, 2004.

U.S. Navy. *The U.S. Navy SEAL Guide to Fitness and Nutrition.* New York: Skyhorse Publishing, 2007.

BIBILIOGRAPHY

"JSOTF-P Assists in Rescue Efforts During Manila Flooding," www.navy.mil/search/display.asp?story_id=48618 (20 May 2010).

Navy SEALs, "Marines Extend Help in Philippines," blog.usnavyseals.com/2009/10/navy-seals-marines-extend-help-in-the-philippines.html#back%23back (20 May 2010).

New York Times, "In Battle, Hunches Prove to Be Valuable," www.nytimes.com/2009/07/28/health/research/28brain.html?pagewanted=2&_r=1&sq=navy%20seals%20AND%20iraq&st=cse&scp=12 (20 May 2010).

"Operation Red Wing," www.navy.mil/moh/mpmurphy/soa.html (20 May 2010).

President Bush's Afghanistan Speech, www.putlearningfirst.com/language/20rhet/bushat.html (20 May 2010).

The Washington Post, "Soul Survivor," www.washingtonpost.com/wpdyn/content/article/2007/06/10/AR2007061001492.html (20 May 2010).

INDEX

PICTURE CREDITS

U.S. Airforce: p. 69
U.S. Army Center of Military History: p. 25
U.S. Department of Defense: pp. 27, 73
   LCdr. Mike Wood: p. 45
   Mass Communication Specialist 3rd Class Blake R. Midnight: p. 33
   Mass Communication Specialist 2nd Class Erika N. Jones: p. 36
   Petty Officer 2nd Class Kyle D. Gahlau: p. 49
U.S. Marines: pp. 11, 36, 71
U.S. Navy: pp. 8, 14, 18, 20, 21, 28, 30, 33, 39, 42, 45, 46, 49, 50, 53, 55, 61, 64, 66, 76, 82, 84, 87, 88

To the best knowledge of the publisher, all images not specifically credited are in the public domain. If any image has been inadvertently uncredited, please notify Harding House Publishing Service, 220 Front Street, Vestal, New York 13850, so that credit can be given in future printings.

ABOUT THE AUTHOR

Jack Montana lives in upstate New York with his wife and three dogs. He writes on military survival, health, and wellness. He graduated from Binghamton University.

ABOUT THE CONSULTANT

Colonel John Carney, Jr. is USAF-Retired, President and the CEO of the Special Operations Warrior Foundation.